YOUR KNOWLEDGE HAS VALUE

Christian Stöhr

Intercultural Communication (China)

GRIN Verlag

Bibliografische Information der Deutschen Nationalbibliothek:

Die Deutsche Bibliothek verzeichnet diese Publikation in der Deutschen National-
bibliografie; detaillierte bibliografische Daten sind im Internet über http://dnb.d-
nb.de/ abrufbar.

Imprint:

Copyright © 2011 GRIN Verlag GmbH
Druck und Bindung: Books on Demand GmbH, Norderstedt Germany
ISBN: 978-3-656-05498-6

This book at GRIN:

http://www.grin.com/en/e-book/182144/intercultural-communication-china

Intercultural Communication

China

Hausarbeit

19.10.2011

Christian Stöhr

Index

„成功与否取决于先前的准备，并没有这样的准备是肯定要失败"

„Success depends upon previous preparation, and without such preparation there is sure to be failure"

Confucius (* 551 BC; † 479 BC)

1. Introduction

The increasing internationalization and globalization has made international competence more significant than ever before. People have to travel around the whole world to find international partners, create business connections and optimize their profits. To do so, people have to study and analyze their new partners from the other side of the globe and need to conceive what they want. Companies working together but each located in other cultural areas need to understand each other. For that reason, both culture A and culture B have to come into contact. Great business connections are the key to success and maximized profits. In order to care for good business connections, the business partners have to accommodate each other to create some kind of harmony. Both partners have to use the right way of Intercultural communication not to mess up these connections.

But, what is Intercultural Communication? For short, Intercultural Communication is the wordless language at cultural contact.[1] The Intercultural Communication deals with the nonverbal communication between people, often business people, from different countries. The spoken language doesn't matter a great deal at our communicative behavior. The nonverbal communication delivers around 65 percent of social meanings between two interlocutors, what is proven by studies.[2] Communication doesn't mean only spoken language. Communication deals with all our senses. It means vision, hearing, feeling and tasting. This is the so called "Metacommunication"[3]. Communication never stops. Meaning if someone stopped talking, his face, his hands, his body continues further sending signals and symbols.[4] Even the clothing is able to do so. For example a fine suit always tells about someone's character or reveals the reasons why the person is dressed that decent. Maybe the person tries to appear serious and wants to make business. Whereas a guy with casualwear or sportswear sends way other signals. So the message is, that our communication doesn't happen one dimensional throughout our spoken language, it mostly happens on way upper dimensions, meaning all actions which get noticed by our counterparts. Comparing to the model of the Culture Iceberg, understanding a culture doesn't only happen on the visible level, to the contrary, it mostly happens on the unseen levels below the water surface.

The term "intercultural" defines that different cultures meet each other. Cultures definitely are different, so any culture has its own ways to interpret situations. Like already mentioned, a great part of communication happens on a nonverbal level. The point is that cultures always differ on that nonverbal level because each culture is bound to a different opinion of actions happening at the nonverbal level. So people from different countries with different

---

[1]Vgl. Heide Wahrlich (2002) von *nibis.de*. Abgerufen am 21. 10. 2011 von
http://www.nibis.de/~iakm/Materialen/wahrlich.pdf Seite 2
[2]Siehe Fußnote 1 Seite 2
[3]Siehe Fußnote 1 Seite 2
[4]Siehe Fußnote 1 Seite 2

cultures have a conversation sending signals while talking. These signals like gestures or body contacts are assimilated on different ways.

For example in Argentina business people talk to each other keeping only a really small distance to the dialogue partner. Their bodies nearly seem to touch while discussing. Confronting a German business man with an Argentinian one in Argentina, the German guy (not knowing anything about Intercultural Communication) would estimate this Argentinian man as really intrusive, moving backwards, gaining distance. The Argentinian business man would try to catch up that distance because he trusts in business, only working on a personal base. This example shows that two different cultures think completely different about contact while discussing serious things.[5]

Without analyzing and understanding other cultures people may never come to an agreement. Before we approach to analyzing or even understanding a culture, we have to define what culture really is.

Culture isn't just a term to be explained in a few phrases. Culture has its own subjective definition that differs from person to person. In 1952 two anthropologists found around 164 different definitions of culture.[6] Many people mix the term "culture" up with "high culture", describing arts, music and architecture. At Intercultural Communication, culture only deals with the parlance of the hidden values of people's culture. Oatey Spencer (1999) defines culture in intercultural studies as the total of attitudes, assumptions, values and principles of everybody's own or principles shared by a group of people, which affect people in that group and their interpretation of other people.[7] Meaning that it is something like an orientation system of a society, that influences noticing, thinking and acting of the people, living in that society.[8]

Summarizing, the Intercultural Communication gets more and more important for contact between cultures that differ extremely. The bigger the differences between culture are, the more it is a challenge for both to deal with each other's culture before debating about may really important deals. In the end the dialogue about the business decides whether it *can make or break the deal.*

---

[5]Vgl. Alexander Groth (2008). *Vorlesung - "Interkulturelle Kommunikation".* Universität Mannheim von http://www.youtube.com/watch?v=DuuRFvtTwgU

[6]Vgl. Stefan Dahl (2000). *intercultural network.* Abgerufen am 22. 10 2011 von http://www.intercultural-network.de/einfuehrung/thema_kultur.shtml

[7]Siehe Fußnote 6

[8]Vgl. Cornelius J.M. Beniers (2005): Managerwissen kompakt: Interkulturelle Kommunikation. Seite 6. Abgerufen am 31.10.2011 von http://bilder.buecher.de/zusatz/14/14176/14176411_lese_1.pdf

2. Regarding China

Regarding China, regarding its history and regarding their geographical vast land area, China isn't just a country; it is another world with different habits and different lifestyles.

Since China has evolved in our nowadays world as an economic superpower, Intercultural Communication, especially for businesses trying to reach the Chinese markets, received more attention than ever before. People have to deal with Chinese mentality and their way of communication. Chinese people differ very much from all the western industrialized countries. About policy, the Chinese have set general equality as an aim. *"The nail that stands out is the nail that gets hammered down."*[9] This saying tells us that the Chinese are not attending individuals but caring about collectivism. The reigning party in China tries to reach the communistic ideas of Mao-Zedong which differ massively to the ideas of any western country.[10] People living in that country identify themselves with all, regardless whether policy or economic ideas, happening and insisting there. People from western countries approaching to reach new markets in China need to know about those circumstances. If people travel to another country, they have to adjust to the people living there to appear friendly and cooperative.

Regarding China, the Confucianism has played a big role in their past as it does nowadays. The Confucianism mainly affects Chinese society, after being mostly abrogated by economic development and modernization. It means that Chinese people really care about family and their relations. They also identify themselves regardless whether in family or at work with hierarchy systems. One of the most important things is the demanding of harmony.[11]

The Chinese people have many factors defining their society that influence the behavior of the people in China very much. These factors are now explained in the following.

2.1 The Guanxi 关系

The term *Guanxi* comprises relationships[12] and personal contact[13] between cooperative partners. In China the *Guanxi* is also understood as a network of all relationships between all cooperatives working together and support each other. The Chinese mentality at work is based on mutuality between the business partners. The people there show this through

---

[9]Vgl. Cornelius J.M. Beniers (2005): Managerwissen kompakt: Interkulturelle Kommunikation. Seite 16. Abgerufen am 31.10.2011 von http://bilder.buecher.de/zusatz/14/14176/14176411_lese_1.pdf
[10]Vgl. wikipedia (2011): Volksrepublik China. Abgerufen am 30.10.2011 von http://de.wikipedia.org/wiki/Volksrepublik_China *Artikel als lesenswert ausgezeichnet!*
[11]Vgl. Yan Slabke-Sun (2009): Interkulturelle Kommunikation China – Einleitung + 1. Guanxi. Abgerufen am 30.10.2011 von http://www.xing.com/net/interkulturelles/asien-189432/interkulturelle-kommunikation-china-einleitung-1-guanxi-23683592/
[12]Vgl. Los Angeles Chinese-School (2011): Chinese Business Culture – Guanxi, An Important Chinese Business Element. Abgerufen am 30.10.2011 von http://chinese-school.netfirms.com/guanxi.html
[13]Siehe Fußnote 9

supporting others voluntarily and regularly and through showing interest for the other's life. So this grants that the partner is morally committed to do things conscientious and well. It is a sign for every man functioning effectively in Chinese society.[14] Meaning that business people from other countries arriving in China to make profit need to know their Chinese partners very well and the other way around. They have to invest sometimes a long time to share interests and to create a mental connection to the new cooperatives. The Chinese people dislike short-lasting connections. They appreciate more than just a few dialogues about the business deal. They want to create a foundation of trust. The manager magazine calls what they don't want the "seagull maneuver", meaning to approach loudly, leave back the mud and fly away back home.[15] The Chinese like to know more about the family, the life and the interests of their partners than it's usual in Europe or somewhere else. The *Guanxi* is the necessary and natural mental base for every business connection.

2.2 The Mianzi 面子

In China, the people always like to show themselves at their best. The reputation of everyone's own is more important than many other things. In the nowadays Chinese society the *Mianzi*, in English *"the face"* is something that you can lose, give someone else or just try to keep for yourself.[16] While living in a society with more than one and a half billion of people it may not be that easy to represent yourself and tell the others (maybe an employer) that YOU are there. You may don't get any attention until you don't have a good *Mianzi*. People always have to watch for their reputation to be successful. As a man of business you always need to look for yourself at first in China. But you also have to care about the others!

The most important principle in China is not to insult the others' *Mianzi*. While being in China you always have to respect any other's dignity not to influence his *Mianzi* in society.[17] Based on Confucians tradition, the harmony in China is classified with a high significance, meaning that keeping this harmony is always good for you and your cooperatives.

Losing your face (*Mianzi*) in China is something like the worst thing that could happen to you. People won't respect you anymore and now less than ever make business with you.[18] Giving up the *Mianzi* is comparable with moral suicide in society, often leading to real suicide.[19]

---

[14]Siehe Fußnote 10

[15]Vgl. Gudrun Weitzenbürger (2007): Erfolg in China -„Alles dreht sich um guanxi". Abgerufen am 30.10.2011 von http://www.manager-magazin.de/unternehmen/karriere/0,2828,457553,00.html

[16]Vgl. Forum China (2010): Mianzi: Das Gesicht verlieren und geben in China. Abgerufen am 31.10.2011 von http://www.forumchina.de/mianzi-gesicht-china

[17]Siehe Fußnote 14

[18]Siehe Fußnote 14

[19]Vgl. Matthias Messmer (2007): China – Schauplätze west-östlicher Begegnungen. Seite 488 Z27f. Abgerufen am 31.10.2011 von http://books.google.de/books?id=Epk2F1MjzvOC&pg=PA488&lpg=PA488&dq=china+gesicht+verlieren+selbstm

Therefore you need to do all possible not to lose your face. As a person coming from other cultural areas with other habits not knowing anything about Chinese *Mianzi* it may not be that hard to lose your face. In Europe it is usual to present your achievements and tell the people how efficiently you're able to work. In contrast to that, people in China would conceive this as pretentious and egoistic. People have to admire and respect the performance of their partners.[20] Talking positively about others may not only increase their reputation, it also strengthens the personal connection, the *Guanxi*, to their mutual advantage.

2.3 Never say "never"!

Like already mentioned, Chinese people really care about consisting harmony in their society. This harmony can be deranged very easily. A Chinese guy may feel insulted if a person negotiates an idea or proposal suggested by him. That's got a reason for sure. In China it is usual that people talking together make use of the high context culture. This term was introduced by E.T. Hall, meaning that people want to keep the much-vaunted harmony and avoid disharmony accrued by direct and sometimes injuring low-context culture negotiations.[21] Some typical high context culture negotiations to keep in mind in China are:[22]

- *"Let us think about this for another time"* (研究 研究 - YanJiu YanJiu) – often used when holding talks to business partners if you are not sure about the trade or don't want to fish or cut bait instantly
- *"It will only take a bit more"* (差不多 - Cha Bu Duo) – often used to express dissatisfaction, telling that you're not really confident with something or something is missing
- *"I've got something left to do"* (有事 - You Shi) – the most used excuse in China, meaning that people say this, when someone for example invites you or wants to undertake something with you and you don't want to seem mean and refuse the invitation – hopefully the one that is inviting you won't ask for further information...
- *"I'm really busy"* (很忙 - Hen Mang) – often used when the person that actually should not ask you about further information after telling him/her that *you've got something left to do* asked after all

---

ord&source=bl&ots=CiYNvc3vDX&sig=zrixrsyuD4spqRfgrv0QFFKGzD0&hl=de&ei=VlKuTvKaPKSL4gSi8v35Dg&sa=X&oi=book_result&ct=result&resnum=4&ved=0CEIQ6AEwAw#v=onepage&q=china%20gesicht%20verlieren%20selbstmord&f=false
[20]Siehe Fußnote 14
[21] Vgl. Yan Slabke-Sun (2009): Interkulturelle Kommunikation China – Einleitung + 1. Guanxi. Abgerufen am 30.10.2011 von Vgl. Yan Slabke-Sun (2009): Interkulturelle Kommunikation China – Einleitung + 1. Guanxi. Abgerufen am 30.10.2011 von http://www.xing.com/net/interkulturelles/asien-189432/interkulturelle-kommunikation-china-einleitung-1-guanxi-23683592/
[22]Siehe Fußnote 21

2.4 Go, get something to eat!

Chinese people attach great importance to get sated while talking to other persons. They understand the act of eating with someone as a great way to create connections, make friends and get something to know about each other[23] (→Guanxi). Being able to eat something good and expansive always tells something about wealth and success in a Chinese people's life. As they invite someone to eat something the Chinese always make an effort on what they present to eat to the guests, because they'd like to receive reputation for their Mianzi.[24] In contrast to German business men, the Chinese don't talk about business in conference rooms, they talk about it while having dinner in a restaurant or having some drinks in a bar. The harmony and small-talk while having lunch or dinner may be more pleasant than only talking about business in meeting rooms.

2.4.1 Greeting

So if you'd like to talk about business, you should invite the Chinese business partners to get something to eat in a restaurant. But you have to consider, that you must be the first being in the restaurant to welcome everyone personally that you have invited to come. Punctuality is a highly respectable virtue in China.[25]

After having greeted your partner the first time you may hand over a present, wrapped in red gift-paper, because the color red stands for fortune in China. Or you hand over some flowers, lilies at best. They stand for harmony.[26] If the Chinese guy hands over a business card to you, take it with both of your hands, read through it carefully and then, after having thanked for it, put it in your wallet very gently.[27]

2.4.2 At the table

At first, the most important guests have to get seated next to the host. While talking to the others, always put their profession in front of their names (like "Manager Chang").[28] Further, in contrast to European culture, it is really usual for Chinese people to behave very rude while having a meal. So don't look disgusted if the man or woman who's just talking to you not having swallowed his or her lunch yet. For Chinese, "bad" table manners like eructating tell the host that they really enjoy the meal. In difference to European restaurants, in China

---

[23]Vgl. Yan Slabke-Sun (2009): Interkulturelle Kommunikation China – 3. Essen und Trinken. Abgerufen am 03.11.2011 von http://www.xing.com/net/interkulturelles/asien-189432/interkulturelle-kommunikation-china-3-essen-und-trinken-24114357/

[24]Siehe Fußnote 23

[25]Vgl. Jens Jahn (2010): Interkulturelle Kompetenz: Geschäftsessen in China. Abgerufen am 06.11.2011 von http://diversity.anythingabout.net/article/interkulturelle-kompetenz-geschaftsessen-in-china/

[26]Vgl. Wolfgang Odendahl (2009): Interkulturelle Verhaltensregeln für Deutsche in chinesischsprachigen Ländern. Abgerufen am 06.11.2011 von http://www.chinalink.de/reisen/verhalten_de.html

[27]Vgl. Alexander Freiherr Knigge (2009): Business-Knigge – China. Abgerufen am 06.11.2011 von http://www.knigge.de/archiv/artikel/der-auslands-knigge-7078.htm

[28]Siehe Fußnote 16

there are many different meals standing in the middle of the table. Everyone orders a few dishes and everyone eats across the whole table.[29]

While eating, you are able to indulge your business partners very easily:

- Neither beat your chopsticks against your bowl nor on the table. Only Chinese beggars do so, that means that you are corrupt.
- Don't point on anybody with your chopsticks.
- Never put your chopsticks vertical in your meals, this is a sign for a sacrifice for the dead.
- Don't hand something on to somebody with your chopsticks. This is a Buddhistic rite of taking bones out of a corpse to hand them over to the relatives.
- If you've been invited by a superior, he will pay. Don't struggle for the decision of who's paying because he's doing something for his reputation (→ *Mianzi*)
- Don't empty the bowles on the table. The host would consider this as an affront, because he would understand it as there was not enough to eat
- Don't eat too fast, it could transition into rush. Your aim was to talk about business while eating, so things should not get rushed

Meaning you have to avoid all those situations[30] if you want to make the deal happen that you wanted to talk about while eating.

2.4.3 Finishing the meeting

After having a great meal with your new partners (hopefully) you may have some drinks in a bar or in a club. Just try to improve your connections to your business partners and care for your Guanxi. If your partners have invited you to the meal, just also invite them for a meal in the future, because this is a friendly gesture improving your Guanxi.[31]

3. What we have learned …

In the end, the Intercultural Communication is besides business conditions the unforeseen factor that plays such an unbelievable big role in making business in different cultural areas. Without having dealt with the culture in a country a business man has to travel to, he may just get rejected and will come back without having any success. Unless regarding business, everyone has to develop intercultural competences for their selves to deal with any foreign culture, because the world gets linked together more and more in the future and people from different cultures meet on each other more often. To avoid any controversies, all of the people in the world have to understand and accept other cultures to coexist peacefully.

---

[29]Vgl. Jens Jahn (2010): Interkulturelle Kompetenz: Geschäftsessen in China. Abgerufen am 06.11.2011 von http://diversity.anythingabout.net/article/interkulturelle-kompetenz-geschaftsessen-in-china/
[30]Vgl. http://www.chinapur.de/html/fettnapfchen.html + Siehe Fußnote 26 + Siehe Fußnote 28
[31]Siehe Fußnote 28

4. Sources

Heide Wahrlich (2002) von *nibis.de*. Abgerufen am 21. 10. 2011 von
http://www.nibis.de/~iakm/Materialen/wahrlich.pdf

Alexander Groth (2008). *Vorlesung - "Interkulturelle Kommunikation"*. Universität Mannheim
von http://www.youtube.com/watch?v=DuuRFvtTwgU

Stefan Dahl (2000). *intercultural network*. Abgerufen am 22. 10 2011 von http://www.intercultural-network.de/einfuehrung/thema_kultur.shtml

Cornelius J.M. Beniers (2005): Managerwissen kompakt: Interkulturelle Kommunikation. Seite 6. Abgerufen am 31.10.2011 von http://bilder.buecher.de/zusatz/14/14176/14176411_lese_1.pdf

wikipedia (2011): Volksrepublik China. Abgerufen am 30.10.2011
vonhttp://de.wikipedia.org/wiki/Volksrepublik_China *Artikel als lesenswert ausgezeichnet!*

Yan Slabke-Sun (2009): Interkulturelle Kommunikation China – Einleitung + 1. Guanxi. Abgerufen am 30.10.2011 von http://www.xing.com/net/interkulturelles/asien-189432/interkulturelle-kommunikation-china-einleitung-1-guanxi-23683592/

Los Angeles Chinese-School (2011): Chinese Business Culture – Guanxi, An Important Chinese Business Element. Abgerufen am 30.10.2011 von http://chinese-school.netfirms.com/guanxi.html

Gudrun Weitzenbürger (2007): Erfolg in China -„Alles dreht sich um guanxi". Abgerufen am 30.10.2011 von http://www.manager-magazin.de/unternehmen/karriere/0,2828,457553,00.html

Forum China (2010): Mianzi: Das Gesicht verlieren und geben in China. Abgerufen am
31.10.2011 von http://www.forumchina.de/mianzi-gesicht-china

Matthias Messmer (2007): China – Schauplätze west-östlicher Begegnungen. Seite 488 Z27f.
Abgerufen am 31.10.2011 von
http://books.google.de/books?id=Epk2F1Mjzv0C&pg=PA488&lpg=PA488&dq=china+gesicht
+verlieren+selbstmordselbstmord&source=bl&ots=CiYNvc3vDX&sig=zrixrsyuD4spqRfgrv0QF
FKGzD0&hl=de&ei=VIKuTvKaPKSL4gSi8v35Dg&sa=X&oi=book_result&ct=result&resnum=4&
ved=0CEIQ6AEwAw#v=onepage&q=china%20gesicht%20verlieren%20selbstmord&f=false

Jens Jahn (2010): Interkulturelle Kompetenz: Geschäftsessen in China. Abgerufen am 06.11.2011 von http://diversity.anythingabout.net/article/interkulturelle-kompetenz-geschaftsessen-in-china/

Wolfgang Odendahl (2009): Interkulturelle Verhaltensregeln für Deutsche in
chinesischsprachigen Ländern. Abgerufen am 06.11.2011 von
http://www.chinalink.de/reisen/verhalten_de.html

Alexander Freiherr Knigge (2009): Business-Knigge – China. Abgerufen am 06.11.2011 von
http://www.knigge.de/archiv/artikel/der-auslands-knigge-7078.htm

http://www.chinapur.de/html/fettnapfchen.html

.